I See Honey Bees

By Julia Jaske

 I see a honey bee.

I see a honey bee swarm.

 I see a honey bee feeling.

I see a honey bee exploring.

6 I see a honey bee working.

I see a honey bee flying.

I see a honey bee sharing.

I see a honey bee drinking.

I see a honey bee collecting.

I see a honey bee smelling.

I see a honey bee resting.

I see a honey bee saying hello!

Word List

honey	sharing
bee	drinking
swarm	collecting
feeling	smelling
exploring	resting
working	saying
flying	hello

I see a honey bee.

I see a honey bee swarm.

I see a honey bee feeling.

I see a honey bee exploring.

I see a honey bee working.

I see a honey bee flying.

I see a honey bee sharing.

I see a honey bee drinking.

I see a honey bee collecting.

I see a honey bee smelling.

I see a honey bee resting.

I see a honey bee saying hello!

CHERRY BLOSSOM PRESS

Published in the United States of America by Cherry Lake Publishing Group
Ann Arbor, Michigan
www.cherrylakepublishing.com

Book Designer: Melinda Millward

Photo Credits: ©manfredxy/Shutterstock.com, front cover, 1, 11; ©Daniel Prudek/Shutterstock.com, back cover, 14; ©Jennifer Bosvert/Shutterstock.com, 2; ©teerapat tongraar/Shutterstock.com, 3; ©sumikophoto/Shutterstock.com, 4; ©RUKSUTAKARN studio/Shutterstock.com, 5; ©BigBlueStudio/Shutterstock.com, 6; ©0 Lorenzo Bernini 0/Shutterstock.com, 7; ©Barnaby Chambers/Shutterstock.com, 8; ©Kostiantyn Kravchenko/Shutterstock.com, 9; ©Mr. Background/Shutterstock.com, 10; ©ETgohome/Shutterstock.com, 12; ©Physics_joe/Shutterstock.com, 13

Cherry Blossom Press is an imprint of Cherry Lake Publishing Group.

Library of Congress Cataloging-in-Publication Data

Names: Jaske, Julia, author.
Title: I see honey bees / by Julia Jaske.
Description: Ann Arbor, Michigan : Cherry Lake Publishing, 2022. | Series: Bugs in my backyard | Audience: Grades K-1
Identifiers: LCCN 2021036407 (print) | LCCN 2021036408 (ebook) | ISBN 9781534198838 (paperback) | ISBN 9781668901410 (pdf) | ISBN 9781668905739 (ebook)
Subjects: LCSH: Honeybee—Juvenile literature.
Classification: LCC QL568.A6 J37 2022 (print) | LCC QL568.A6 (ebook) | DDC 595.79/9—dc23
LC record available at https://lccn.loc.gov/2021036407
LC ebook record available at https://lccn.loc.gov/2021036408

Cherry Lake Publishing Group would like to acknowledge the work of the Partnership for 21st Century Learning, a Network of Battelle for Kids. Please visit http://www.battelleforkids.org/networks/p21 for more information.

Printed in the United States of America
Corporate Graphics

Say hello to CHERRY BLOSSOM PRESS books!

Each A level reader features a whole language approach to literacy, with colorful art and photographs to encourage little readers.

This series utilizes a combination of sight words and repetition that builds recognition and confidence. Bold, colorful photographs correlate directly to the text to help guide readers through the book.

Read all the books in the Bugs in My Backyard series!

I See Ants

I See Butterflies

I See Dragonflies

I See Fireflies

I See Honey Bees

I See Ladybugs

I See Moths

I See Walking Sticks

GRL: A

ISBN-13: 978-1-5341-9883-8

CHERRY BLOSSOM PRESS